D1711844

SPACE!

VENUS

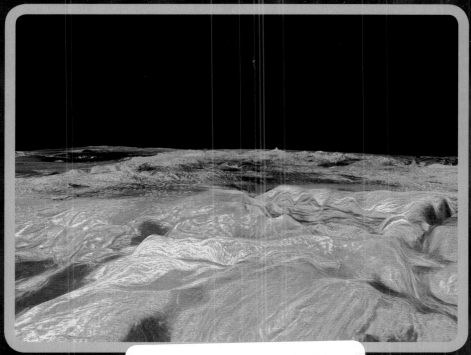

RUTH BJORKLUND

mc **Marshall Cavendish**
Benchmark
New York

Marshall Cavendish Benchmark
99 White Plains Road
Tarrytown, New York 10591
www.marshallcavendish.us

Library of Congress Cataloging-in-Publication Data
Bjorklund, Ruth.
  Venus / by Ruth Bjorklund.
    p. cm. -- (Space!)
  Summary: "Describes Venus, including its history, its composition, and its role in the
solar system"--Provided by publisher.
  Includes bibliographical references and index.
  ISBN 978-07614-4251-6
  1. Venus (Planet)--Juvenile literature. I. Title.
  QB621.B52 2010
  523.42--dc22
  2009014665

Editor: Karen Ang
Publisher: Michelle Bisson
Art Director: Anahid Hamparian
Series Design by Daniel Roode
Production by nSight, Inc.

Front cover: Detlev van Ravenswaay / Photo Researchers Inc.
Title page: A computerized image of part of Venus's surface.
Photo research by Candlepants, Incorporated
Front cover: Photo Researchers Inc.
The photographs in this book are used by permission and through the courtesy of:
Super Stock: Digital Images Ltd., 1, 7. Getty Images: Roz Woodward, 4, 5; The Bridgeman
Art Library, 16; Jim Ballard, 34, 35; World Perspectives, 51; Guang Niu, 54. Photo
Researchers Inc.: Detlev van Ravenswaay, 6; Mark Garlick, 12; John Chumack, 23; Science
Source, 24, 25; Christian Darkin, 52. NASA: "Courtesy of SOHO. SOHO is a project of
international cooperation between ESA and NASA." 8; JPL/DLR, 10; JPL, 26, 27, 31, 32,
58, 39, 41, 42, 43, 45; JPL/USGS, 36; NSSDC, 48. AP Images: Mahesh Kumar A, 14, 15;
Daytona Beach News-Journal, Jim Tiller, 21; Itsuo Inouye, 22; Novosti, 28; 29; 30; ESA-
AOES Medialab, 33. Art Resource, NY: Bildarchiv Preussischer Kulturbesitz, 17. The
Image Works: World History/Topham, 19. Corbis: Will & Demi McIntyre, 55; NASA/Roger
Ressmeyer, 56. Illustration on page 11 by Mapping Specialists © Marshall Cavendish
Corporation.
Printed in Malaysia
123456

CONTENTS

1

THE SOLAR SYSTEM

Scientists think that the universe is about 13 billion years old. The Sun and its Solar System came into existence more than 4 billion years ago. The Sun was created from an enormous cloud made up of gases, such as cold hydrogen, and interstellar medium (ISM), which is **cosmic** dust and particles. The nearby explosion of a massive star, called a **supernova**, upset the cloud, which then sent the various particles colliding into one another. The collisions caused the particles to clump together into small masses. The clumps continued to build up and created energy that turned the cold, static and shapeless cloud into a hot, spinning sphere. The sphere—called a proto-solar nebula— flattened into a disk with a bulge in the center. The Sun was born from that bulge.

Our Solar System most likely formed when a supernova similar to this one exploded, causing a chain of events that lead to the formation of the Sun and planets.

THE PLANETS

The Sun was originally much hotter than it is today. As it cooled, the remaining dust, gas, metals, and other particles spun out and away to form small bodies called planetesimals. Some scientists theorize that some of the planetesimals accumulated enough gas, ice, and particles to become big enough to form planets. The innermost of these planets—Mercury, Venus, Earth, and Mars—took in gas and ice, as well as minerals, such as silicon and magnesium. Mercury, the planet closest to the Sun and the hottest planet, took in mostly metal. Earth and Venus collected metals to form their heated cores, or centers, and dirt particles to form their rocky crusts, or outermost layers. Ice crystals made from frozen water, ammonia, or other compounds bombarded Earth and the other planets. Beyond the

After the Sun formed 4.5 billion years ago, orbiting space materials, such as rocks, minerals, and gases, developed into the planets, comets, asteroids, and other celestial bodies.

inner planets is a swirling belt of rocky objects called asteroids. The asteroid belt revolves around the Sun between Mars and the outer planets.

The masses that developed into planets beyond the asteroid belt are farther from the Sun and colder. These bodies collected huge amounts of gas compounds containing cold methane, ammonia, and ice. The rocky and icy cores of these planetary bodies began to pull in hydrogen and helium. Jupiter, the largest of all the planets in our Solar System, developed into a mass twice as large as all the rest of the planets combined. Next in size is Saturn. Both of these

Neptune, one of the gas giants, appears to be a greenish blue color because of the methane in the planet's atmosphere.

planets, known as "gas giants" are composed of mostly hydrogen and helium. Beyond Saturn, Neptune and Uranus formed into icy, hydrogen-wrapped planets. All of the four distant planets are surrounded in rings made of ice and rock particles that form naturally occurring satellites called moons.

ENERGY FROM THE SUN

All of the planets orbit the Sun and receive or reflect its energy and light. The Sun's energy comes from an atomic reaction that changes hydrogen into helium. In the extreme heat of the Sun's inner core, hydrogen atoms compress, or fuse, to form helium. But the helium is a smaller, lighter atom, so there is extra mass left over. The excess from the hydrogen fusion is released as nuclear energy. It is estimated that every second, the Sun converts 700,000,000 tons (722,343,836 tonnes) of hydrogen into 695,000,000 tons (706,152,602 tonnes) of helium and 5,000,000 tons (5,080,235 tonnes) of energy in the form of gamma rays. (Gamma rays are invisible rays that carry energy.) The energy travels outward toward the planets where it is absorbed and reflected.

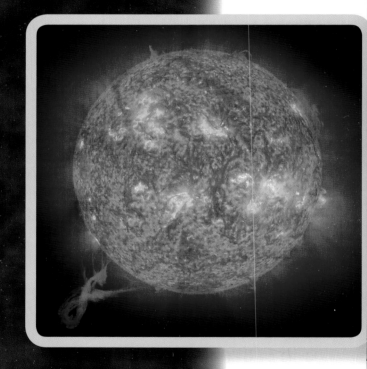

For many decades, our Solar System was made up of nine major planets. Since 2006, however, Pluto—once known as the smallest and farthest planet—has been considered a dwarf planet. It does not have several important features that the other eight planets have and was reclassified as a smaller type of celestial, or space, body.

Gravity

Gravity played a central role in forming the Solar System. Gravity is the force that attracts one object to another. The larger the size of an object, the greater gravitational force it will have on smaller surrounding objects. When the proto-solar nebula was forming, the gases were cold and they had little effect on the surrounding space particles. Eventually, the gases heated up and the particles began to attract one another and collect into masses. As the masses grew larger they began pulling at each other with growing gravitational force. This force caused greater heat and produced a spinning effect. Had there been no gravitational force, the particles that formed into planetesimals and planets, would have traveled away from the Sun. But because the Sun is much larger than all of the planetary objects in its Solar System, it is able to pull the objects inward. Rather than hurtling through outer space, the planets are forced by gravity to revolve in an orbit around the Sun.

MOONS

While the Solar System was developing, rocks, ice crystals, and smaller planetesimals moved through space, sometimes slamming into planets and releasing storms of debris. One impact in particular occurred approximately 4.5 billion years ago. A huge rocky object crashed into Earth. The object's heat melted Earth's surface, sending fragments into space. The fragments cooled into a round ball. It then went into **orbit** around Earth. This is how the Moon formed. Many other moons of the other planets were formed in a similar way, but some of the moons—such as Phobos, a moon of Mars, and Nereid, a

Jupiter has more than sixty known moons. From top to bottom, the moons shown here are Io, Europa, Ganymede, and Callisto.

Mercury, Venus, Earth, and Mars are the terrestrial, or land, planets. Jupiter, Saturn, Uranus, and Neptune are considered gas giants. Pluto, which was once considered a main planet alongside the others, is now known as a dwarf planet.

A computer illustration shows how icy objects probably look as they move around the Kuiper Belt.

moon of Jupiter—are actually orbiting asteroids captured by the planets' gravity. Mercury and Venus do not have moons. All planets except for those two have at least one moon.

BEYOND THE PLANETS

There is another belt of planetary objects orbiting outside of the outermost planets. This is called the **Kuiper Belt**. Pluto is the largest planetary object in the Kuiper Belt. To date, scientists have discovered more than one thousand icy objects spinning at the edge of the Solar System—and there are probably millions more. Astronomers believe the objects in the Kuiper Belt hold the frozen secrets to the ancient building blocks of the Solar System.

Surrounding the entire Solar System is what scientists believe to be a giant spherelike structure called the Oort Cloud. Named after the scientist Jan Oort, the cloud is somewhere between 4 trillion and 9 trillion miles (6 trillion and 14 trillion kilometers) away from the Sun. Comets and asteroids are believed to reside within the Oort Cloud.

Scientists believe there is much more to discover far beyond the Oort Cloud. Perhaps one day technology will allow us to explore the far reaches of the universe and learn more about space and the history and origins of all the objects within it.

2

DISCOVERING VENUS

Since ancient times, Venus has been a known object in the sky. Due to its nearness to Earth, Venus can be seen without the help of a telescope or satellite. Other than the Sun or the full Moon, Venus is the brightest object in Earth's night sky.

At certain times during the year, Venus appears in our evening sky when the planet is on the eastern side of the Sun. It appears in the morning sky when it is on the western side of the Sun. As a result, many ancient cultures believed that Venus was not one object but two. They called the one they saw at sunrise the morning star and the one they could see at sunset, the evening star.

This view of Venus (upper left) and a crescent Moon (lower right) was seen from India in 2007.

VENUS

The planet was worshipped by many early societies, such as the ancient Romans, Sumerians, Greeks, and people of the Middle East, who associated it with their goddesses of beauty or love. However, other societies felt that because Venus disappeared from the sky for months at a time, it represented the dark gods of the mysterious underworld.

Early civilizations did not have telescopes, satellites, or space missions to help them understand the objects in space. But they still managed to observe the features and movement of the objects in the sky. Many cultures based their beliefs and traditions on the stars and planets in space.

In the region that now includes present-day Central and South America,

A marble statue of Venus, or Aphrodite, as she was known in Greek mythology.

ancient Mayan and Aztec astronomers based their 260-day yearly calendar on the orbit of the object we call Venus when it was visible on Earth. To this day, that type of calendar is used in some parts of Guatemala. In the Mayan creation story called the *Popul Vuh*, Mayan astronomers described the movements of Venus and were able to predict exactly when and where it would appear in the sky. By studying the planet's patterns, the Mayans could predict their seasons—specifically when rain would fall. They would plan their crop planting and harvesting based on those observations.

Around 1600 BCE, in ancient Babylonia—now the home of present-day Iraq—astronomers recognized that the morning star and the evening star were the same object. They also noted that the reason Venus, which they called Ishtar, was not visible during the day was that it was close to the Sun.

An ancient Mayan artifact shows illustrations of the different phases of Venus (left) alongside images of Mayan gods (right).

THE CENTER OF THE SOLAR SYSTEM

In some ancient civilizations, astronomers—such as Hipparchus, Ptolemy, and Aristotle—believed that the Sun, Moon, and planets revolved around Earth. For hundreds of years, people agreed with the theory that Earth was the center of everything.

Nicolaus Copernicus, a Polish astronomer born in 1473, proposed a theory arguing that the planets revolved around the Sun. This is known as a heliocentric theory. (*Helios* is the Greek word for the Sun). Copernicus also said that the Earth rotated on an **axis**, explaining the occurrence of day and night. Copernicus noted that Mercury and Venus never moved more than a certain distance from the Sun, suggesting that the planets moved around the Sun in a circular pattern. His radical views disturbed government and religious leaders. They did not want people to believe that Earth was not the center of the universe. However, Copernicus's science was so accurate and simple that eventually his theories were more broadly accepted.

In the early part of the seventeenth century, one of the first telescopes was made. It allowed the user to see a space object magnified three times. Soon after, an Italian scientist named Galileo Galilei developed a telescope that magnified objects up to twenty times. With his telescope, Galileo observed the Sun, Moon,

A chart from the 1700s depicts the Copernican heliocentric, or Sun-centered, view of the Solar System.

and the planets. He studied the phases, or different appearances, of Venus, from the time it changed from a bright orb to a crescent to a darker shape. Galileo believed that these visible changes were a result of the amount of sunlight reflecting off of Venus. He thought that this proved Copernicus's theory that the planets revolved around the Sun in a relatively circular orbit.

A German astronomer named Johannes Kepler published a work that came to be known as the *Three Laws of Planetary Motion*. In it, Kepler explained that the planets did not orbit in a circular path, but in an **elliptical** one.

THE TRANSIT OF VENUS

In 1619, Kepler used his laws to determine the distances from the planets to the Sun. He was aware that his calculations could become more specific by using information gathered during a **transit** of Venus. A transit is a similar to an eclipse. An eclipse is an event where a celestial object moves into the shadow of another. One example is a solar eclipse, which occurs when Earth moves into the shadow created by the Moon coming between Earth and the Sun. A transit, however, is when a celestial body passes in front of another and appears to move across it. Using geometric calculations and his belief in elliptical orbits, Kepler determined the position of the planets. He predicted that on December 6, 1631, Venus would make a transit across the face of the Sun. If the planet did as he suspected, then it would prove many of his calculations. He also asked other scientists to watch carefully, because if Venus did pass in front of the Sun, they would be able to determine the diameter of the planet. Unfortunately, Kepler died in 1630 and never knew that his predictions were correct.

In 1677, a follower of Kepler, Edmond Halley (after whom Halley's Comet is named), predicted another transit of Venus for the years 1761 and 1769. He encouraged scientists to use geometry to study the transit in order to measure the distance between Earth and the Sun. During the transit of Venus in 1761, scientists noted for the first time that Venus must have a dense

When it is in transit, Venus appears as a small dark dot against the giant yellow Sun.

atmosphere because they could see a blurry halo around the planet. For both transit years, European governments sent explorers to all points of the globe. The explorers were asked to use special telescopes to watch and time the transit of Venus from their position. Using the information gathered by the explorers, scientists determined that the distance to the Sun from Earth was roughly 95 million miles, which is very close to today's measurement of 92,955,807.267 miles (149,597,870.691 km).

Though occurring quite close to each other in the eighteenth century, transits of Venus are quite rare. They occurred in 1639, 1761, 1769, 1874, 1882, and 2004. The next transit will occur on June 2012. What is the pattern of these numbers? Halley, Kepler and other scientists noted that the orbit of Venus is tilted slightly in respect to Earth's orbit. As a result, when viewed from Earth,

VENUS

Venus appears above or below the Sun most of the time. But when the two planets are on almost the same plane, or lined up, then the transit of Venus is visible on Earth. The first recorded transit of Venus in 1639 was 121.5 years from the next. The following transit was 8 years later. After that, the next one was 105.5 years later, followed by another transit 8 years later. This odd pattern of numbers remains constant and repeats every 243 years so that there are four transits of Venus every 243 years. Based on history and calculations, **NASA (National Aeronautics and Space Administration**) prepared a database that is a record of the transits of Venus. The database marks transits from the past to predictions for the future, from 2000 BCE to 4000 CE.

Transits of Venus have been very useful to the study of astronomy. Not only were they historically important in scientific discovery, but today they enable astronomers to study how a transit behaves, helping them to accurately observe objects in transit beyond our Solar System.

Students watch a projection of Venus in transit across the Sun. The safest way to view the Sun without looking directly at it, which could damage your eyes, is through the projection method, which uses a telescope to project an image of the Sun on a white surface.

VIEWING VENUS FROM EARTH

Venus is closer to the Sun than Earth, so Venus's orbit around the Sun covers a shorter distance. (It takes Venus about 224 Earth days to pass around the Sun, in comparison to Earth's 365 days.) Because the two planets travel in the same direction, Venus appears in the sky for 260 days. Once Venus is visible to us on Earth, it takes another 584 days for Venus to return to the same place in the sky.

At the time when Venus comes closest to Earth, its light becomes brighter, while its shape grows smaller. The planet appears to be changing from a large, round orb to a slender crescent.

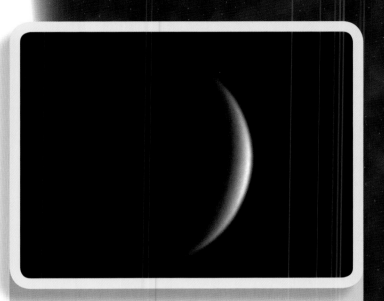

Venus sometimes appears as a thin crescent, much like the Moon.

During the 260 days when it is visible in the sky, Venus appears in the evening sky when it is on the eastern side of the Sun. It appears in the morning sky when it is on the western side of the Sun.

3

MISSIONS TO VENUS

There have been more successful space missions to Venus than to any other planet. The first successful spacecraft mission to another planet involved *Mariner 2,* a type of space **probe**. It was bound for Venus and launched on August 27, 1962. Scientists at NASA's Jet Propulsion Laboratory (JPL) were successful in creating technology that allowed two-way radio wave communication between the spacecraft and the laboratory. Engineers were also able to control the spacecraft's path. After it launched, *Mariner 2* blasted past Earth's gravitational pull and went into orbit around the Sun. Much of its power came from solar panels that drew energy from the Sun.

This image of Venus is from the *Mariner 10* spacecraft, which was the first spacecraft to provide close-up images of Venus and Mercury.

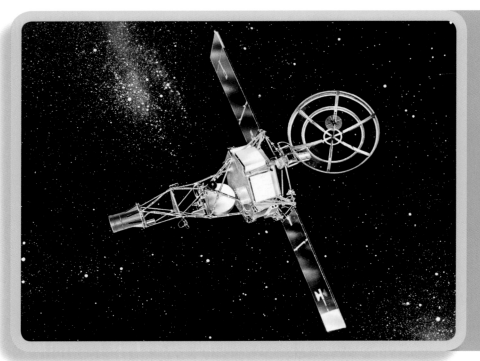

The *Mariner 2* mission provided scientists with the first recorded temperatures on Venus.

    It took *Mariner 2* three-and-a-half months to come close to Venus. On December 14, 1962, it came closest to the planet—about 21,000 miles (34,000 km). Before it resumed its orbit around the Sun, the probe took three important scans. Using its radio capabilities, it sent back data about Venus's surface temperature and cloud cover. Scientists discovered that the surface temperature of Venus was at least 790 degrees Fahrenheit (425 degrees Celsius). *Mariner 2* also helped them discover that Venus rotated slowly in a retrograde motion—meaning clockwise. *Mariner 2*'s observations also noted that Venus's cloud cover extended about 50 miles (80 km) above the planet's surface.

MORE *MARINER* AND *VENERA* MISSIONS

After *Mariner 2*'s historic mission, Russian scientists launched a Venus-bound space probe, named *Venera 4,* in June 1967. In October of the same year, *Venera 4* entered the dense atmosphere of Venus. It released various devices, such as thermometers, gas analyzers, and other meters measuring magnetic fields and cosmic rays. The spacecraft sent back signals for ninety-four minutes until contact was lost.

Soon after, the United States launched another *Mariner* **flyby** mission named *Mariner 5. Mariner 5* sent back signals about Venus as well as data about magnetic fields, particles, and the release of ultraviolet rays.

Mariner 5 was launched from Cape Canaveral, Florida in June 1967.

Venera 9, shown here in a small-scale model, transmitted the very first black and white images of Venus.

Between 1969 and 1975, there were five more *Venera* missions to Venus. *Venera 7* was the first spacecraft to land on Venus and though the signal was very weak, for 23 minutes it sent back information about the planet's high temperature and atmospheric pressure. *Venera 8* sent back information about light on Venus, which is comparable to light on Earth on a very cloudy day. This energized scientists because it meant that there was enough light to transmit photographic images from Venus to Earth. In 1975, *Venera 9* sent back the first images of Venus.

In 1973, *Mariner 10* made history by being the first spacecraft to travel to two planets—Venus and Mercury. It also provided the first close-up images of the two planets.

PIONEER VENUS

The next U.S. mission to Venus, called *Pioneer Venus*, included two spacecraft launched separately. The *Pioneer Venus Orbiter* was launched in May 1978. It started orbiting Venus in December of that same year. The orbiter's mission included examining how the planet's clouds were distributed, determining surface characteristics, calculating the gravity field of Venus, and studying the planet's upper atmosphere.

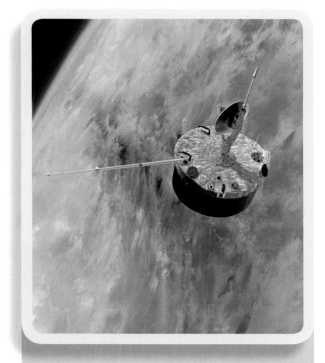

The *Pioneer Venus Multi-Probe* was launched in August 1978. This spacecraft was made up of a "bus" that carried four probes. The probes and the bus were created to study the planet's atmosphere. The probes and the bus entered Venus's atmosphere in December 1978. They examined things such as cloud particles and atmospheric composition.

An artist's version of what *Pioneer Venus* looked like as it orbited Venus.

VEGA MISSIONS AND BEYOND

The Russian space agency continued to send up more *Venera* orbiters and **landers**, while the United States began a new series of missions called *Vega*. *Vega 1* and *2* orbited Venus and flew by Halley's Comet as it entered the Solar System in 1984. *Vega 1* and *2* also projected weather balloons into Venus's atmosphere to study the planet's three-tiered cloud layer.

For four years, beginning in 1990, a U.S. spacecraft named *Magellan* successfully mapped most of the surface of Venus, sending back images that were clearer than anything from earlier missions. The next three U.S. spacecraft to fly by Venus were part of missions to other planets.

The *Magellan* spacecraft was released from the Space Shuttle *Atlantis* in 1989 and began its journey into Venus's orbit.

This illustration shows the path *Magellan* took around Venus. The spacecraft is shown relaying information to Earth (bottom right). The bright star at the top is the Sun.

This computer-generated image of part of Venus's surface was created based on the images sent back by the *Magellan* spacecraft.

From 2005 to 2009, The European Space Agency (ESA) sent a mission to Venus. *Venus Express* was designed to study how heat escapes from Venus and why the atmosphere rotates so much faster than the planet. More importantly, *Venus Express* was designed to study the **greenhouse gas effect** that Venus's thick carbon-dioxide (CO_2) atmosphere creates. These studies are important to Earth's future since our planet is also experiencing greenhouse gas effects. *Venus Express* was able to send clear signals and images back to Earth from a distance of 146 million miles (235 million km) away.

An illustration provided by the ESA shows the *Venus Express* as it started orbiting around Venus in 2006.

4

FEATURES OF VENUS

Venus has dense layers of clouds in its atmosphere. As a result, using optical telescopes from Earth—even powerful ones—cannot give a viewer any detailed images of Venus.

Most of our information about the physical features of Venus was provided by satellites in space or by space missions. The missions that entered the atmosphere and traveled to the planet's surface sent detailed information and images that mapped the surface. The collected data reveal that the terrain of the planet is rugged. There are mountains, craters, canyons, ridges, volcanoes, valleys, high plateaus, and large lava plains.

NASA has digitally enhanced this view of Venus, showing one of many lava flows that make up the surface of the planet.

SURFACE FEATURES

Venus has mountains, volcanoes, and highlands, but the planet as a whole is relatively flat. The distance between its highest point and its lowest point is about 8 miles (13 km). On Earth that difference is closer to 12 miles (20 km).

Most of the surface of Venus, approximately 70 percent, is made up of volcanic plains. These plains were most likely formed by lava flow when the planet experienced volcanic activity. About 20 percent of the planet is made of low-lying plains and 10 percent are highlands. The highlands appear to be formed from volcanic surges that rose above the average **elevation**

This image from *Magellan* has been colorized to show the different elevations on Venus.

of the planet. (Heights on Venus are measured in terms of "average global elevation," as there is no sea level, like on Earth, to use as an elevation reference point.) Also rising above the average elevation are three continent-like land masses. The scientific term for these large land masses is **terra**.

VENUSIAN LAND FEATURES

Scientists use special names for the different types of land features on Venus and other celestial bodies. Here are examples of some of them:

DESCRIPTION	SINGULAR NAME	PLURAL
Large highland, similar to a continent	terra	terrae
High plain or plateau	planum	plana
Mountain range	mons	montes
Canyon	chasma	chasmata
Cliff	rupe	rupes
Harsh and rugged area	tessera	tesserae
Oval crown-shaped feature	corona	coronae

Ishtar and Aphrodite Terra

Ishtar Terra is approximately the size of Australia. On the Earth-facing side of Venus, this terra is located in the northern area. It has many unusual and unique characteristics. A massive high plain called the Lakshmi Planum rises more than 2 miles (3 km) above the global average elevation, and covers about 700,000 square miles (1.8 million square km). It is crisscrossed with old lava flows and contains a few volcanic calderas—craters formed after volcanic explosions—the largest being the Sacajawea and the Colette. Ishtar Terra is also covered by an unusual—and unique to Venus—land feature called a tessera. Tesserae (many tessera) such as those named Fortuna, Atropos, and Clotho, are formations that are sharply ridged, grooved, folded, and cracked. Scientists think that tesserae are the oldest visible land formation. They were most likely formed by gravity as huge blocks of nearly liquid rock crashed down mountainsides.

Sharp cliffs, or rupes, form the southern edge of Lakshmi Planum; they are steep and can rise about 2 miles (3 km) high. To the east rises the highest mountain range on Venus, the Maxwell Montes. The highest point is approximately 7.4 miles (12 km). The north, west, and southeastern edges of the Lakshmi Planum are lined with craggy mountain ranges that fall sharply to the plains below.

All of the main mountain ranges are located on Ishtar Terra—Frejya Montes, Akna Montes, and Danu Montes. The mountain

The focus of this image is the eastern edge of the Lakshmi Planum and the western edge of Maxwell Montes. Maxwell Montes is the only Venusian feature to be named after a man. James Maxwell was a highly respected Scottish physicist.

ranges are somewhat similar to Earth's because they also have folds and faults, or breaks in the rock. Flanking the terras are several low plains called planitae.

Planitae tend to be at or below the average elevation. Deep rifts or channels called chasmata can be found slicing through the plains. They resemble dried-up river beds. The longest chasma on the planet is the Hildr Chasma. It is more than 4,200 miles (6,800 km) long, and is often compared in length to Earth's Nile River.

The larger terra, Aphrodite Terra, is near the planet's equator. It is about the size of South America. The west side of Aphrodite Terra contains two large areas. These areas are scarred by tesserae. In the center of the terra, two major chasmata surround a large land feature called the Artemis Corona.

Coronae

Scientists say that coronae (the plural form of corona) are unknown elsewhere in the Solar System. They are a type of landform that is unique to Venus. Coronae resemble craters, but they are nearly perfect ovals with ridges and fault lines spreading outward. Scientists believe coronae are formed by flowing material from the planet's mantle. The mantle of a planet is the thick layer of rock that surrounds the planet's inner core. Above the mantle is the crust, which is a relatively thin crystallized

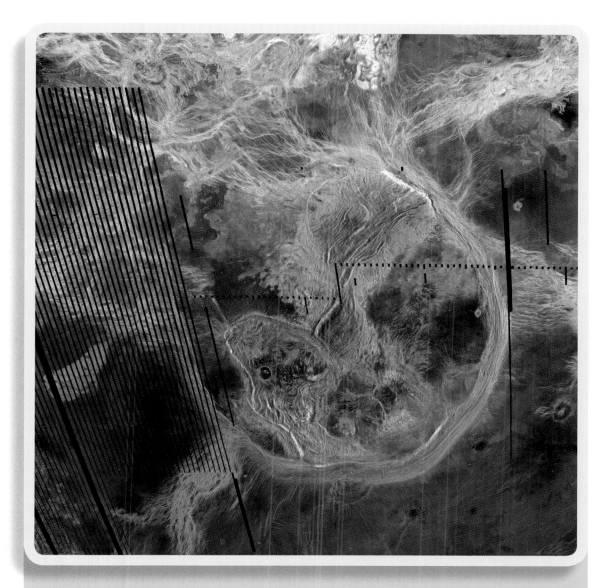

This *Magellan* image shows Artemis Chasma, which encloses the Artemis Corona, the largest known corona on Venus. This corona is so large that the part of the United States that stretches from around Denver all the way to the West Coast would fit inside.

layer made from melted mantle material. The two features combined are called the lithosphere.

Scientists think that Venus's extreme temperatures cause rocks to become viscous, or like thick flowing liquid. Where the lithosphere is thinnest, viscous mantle material pushes upward and causes a bulge. The bulge collapses to form coronae. The Aine Corona is about 186 miles (300 km) across. Lada Terra, the third and most recently named terra, contains several very large coronae.

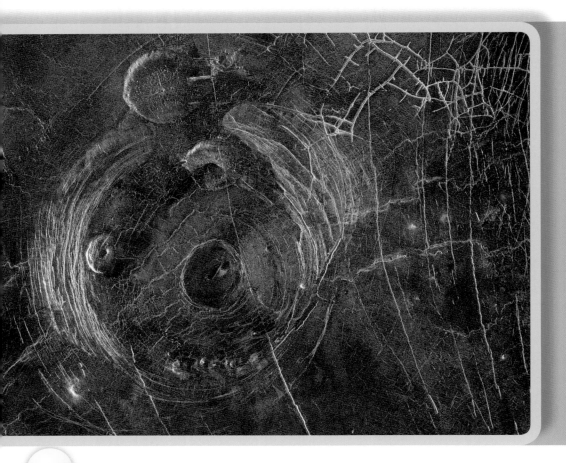

Pancake domes, which are remnants of volcanic activity that look like pancakes, can be seen near Aine Corona.

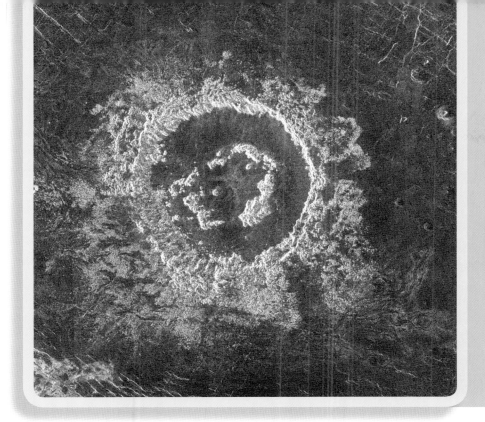

Barton Crater was named after Clara Barton, a famous American nurse who had many accomplishments, including forming the Red Cross.

Craters

Craters are present on Venus and sometimes they are confused with coronae. But craters are jagged and many of them appear to be impact craters. Impact craters are formed when an asteroid or meteorite passes through the planet's atmosphere and crashes to the surface. Because Venus's atmosphere is so thick and the planet is so hot, most asteroids could not withstand the temperatures and were destroyed before striking the planet's surface. Those that survived had to be very large. As a result, small craters are rare on Venus. Few are smaller than 1.9 miles (3 km) across. Mead Crater is the largest impact crater on Venus, located on Aphrodite Terra.

NAMES ON VENUS

The International Astronomical Union (IAU) is responsible for the nomenclature, or scientific naming, of celestial bodies and their features. The IAU tries to ensure diversity by evenly using ethnic, cultural, and national names.

The rules for nomenclature on Venus are specific, with few exceptions. Each geographic formation is labeled with two names: a feature classification, such as terra, region, planum, chasma, or mons; and a female name taken from a particular category, such as Goddesses of War. Some examples of names on Venus are

Goddesses of love that were used to describe a terra:

Examples: *Aphrodite*, Greek goddess of love; *Ishtar*, Babylonian goddess; *Lada*, Slavic goddess of love

Famous historical women used to name large calderas:

Examples: *Mona Lisa*, an Italian merchant's wife painted by Leonardo da Vinci; *Sacajawea* the Native American guide for Lewis and Clark.

Goddesses of hearth and home used to describe a rupe, or cliff:

Examples: *Ut*, Siberian goddess of the hearth fire; *Vesta*, the Roman goddess of hearth and home

Names of deceased women who made history in their professions are used to define craters:

Examples: *Judith Resnik*, an engineer and astronaut, and *Christa McAuliffe*, an astronaut and teacher, both of whom died in the explosion of the Space Shuttle *Challenger* in 1986.

Volcanoes

Venus is known to have thousands of volcanoes. These range from small vents to large shield volcanoes. Shield volcanoes are similar to the Mauna Loa volcano in Hawaii. A shield volcano sits over a hot spot, which is an area where hot, molten rock—called magma—rises up. The magma melts the crust enough to escape and erupt to the surface. However, the similarity to Earth's Mauna Loa ends at this point. This is because of the differences in Earth's and Venus's crusts. Earth's crust shifts as a result of movements called plate tectonics. There is no true evidence that the crust does the same on Venus. So shield volcanoes on Earth eventually move away from their location over the hotspot and go dormant. The shield volcanoes on Venus do not move, so they continue to grow.

Maat Mons is the largest volcano on Venus.

VENUS'S AGE

The ESA's *Venus Express* sent back interesting data about the age of Venus. Scientists studying the planet believe that when planets were first forming, Venus had a head start on Earth and developed very rapidly. They theorize that Venus had volumes of water and oceans. But the carbon dioxide in the atmosphere overtook the planet and Venus's water was lost. Once the planet went dry, its evolution slowed down.

Earth, in the meantime, recycled its carbon dioxide. Sea algae and rocks stored excess carbon dioxide in the oceans and kept it from accumulating in the atmosphere. The water helped the crust form flexible plates. These plates shift and move against and under each other in a system called plate tectonics. Plate tectonics releases and recycles heat and gases, keeping Earth's temperature from becoming extreme. Some scientists believe that Venus is moving toward developing tectonic plate activity. In that case, some of its heat and gases may be reduced.

Most shield volcanoes on Venus expand outward as much as—or more than—upward because the magma of a shield volcano is very liquid and the lava flows a long way before becoming solid rock again. The largest volcano on the planet is found on the eastern side of Aphrodite Terra, in a raised area called Atla Regio. The volcano, known as Maat Mons, is approximately 5 miles (8 km) above the average surface and has a diameter of more than 180 miles (298 km).

Only a few areas of Venus now appear to have active volcanoes. Yet 300 to 500 million years ago, it appears there were massive eruptions throughout the planet. The volcanoes likely covered the surface in lava, covering most evidence of older geologic formations. Scientists believe this because the oldest features scientists have found on Venus seem to be only about 800 million years old. Some rocks found on other planets, like Earth—which formed shortly after Venus—date back 4.8 billion years.

ORBIT

Venus has the most circular orbit of any of the planets in the Solar System. Since it is the second planet from the Sun, Venus's orbit is heavily influenced by the Sun's mighty gravitational pull. As a result, Venus moves swiftly around the Sun, taking only 224.7 Earth days to make a complete revolution. That means that a Venusian year takes about 224.7 Earth days.

On the other hand, Venus spins very slowly on its axis. A single Venusian day is equal to 243 Earth days. (By contrast, an Earth day—from noon to noon—takes 24 hours.) As a result, a day on Venus is longer than a year. Venus rotates on its axis in a clockwise direction. This is different from Earth's rotation, which is counterclockwise. On Venus the Sun rises in the west and sets in the east.

The atmosphere of Venus also rotates in a clockwise motion. But unlike on some other planets, Venus's atmosphere rotates at a different rate from the rest of the planet. The clouds on Venus move nearly sixty times faster than the planet itself. So the atmosphere takes only four Earth days to rotate around the planet's axis.

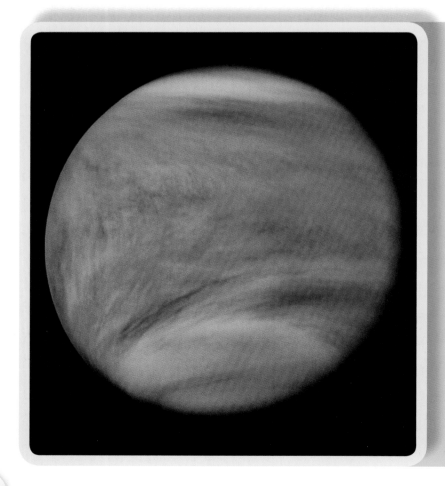

An image taken by the *Pioneer Venus* orbiter shows Venus's cloudy atmosphere.

ATMOSPHERE

Venus has a very dense and very hot atmosphere, with extremely high pressure. The atmospheric pressure—the measure of how much the air is pushing down on a surface—is ninety times greater than that of Earth. The atmosphere of Venus is thicker and the temperature is hotter than any other planet in the Solar System. Despite being twice as far from the Sun as Mercury, Mercury's average temperature is nearly one third of Venus's average temperature.

At the surface, the temperature of Venus is more than 890 degrees Fahrenheit (480 degrees C). The cloud cover on Venus is so thick and the winds close to the surface are so light that there is no temperature difference between day and night. There also is not a large temperature difference between the equators and the poles.

Venus has at least three cloud layers made up of 96 percent carbon dioxide, 3 percent nitrogen, and traces of sulfur dioxide, argon, water, and other vaporized gases. Many astronomers believe that much of Venus's atmosphere was created by volcanoes releasing gases.

The lowest level of clouds extends to about 25 miles (45 km) upward. At this level, the *Venus Express* mission measured wind speeds at 130 miles per hour (210 km per hour). Wind speeds can reach 230 miles per hour (379 km per hour). It also appears that there are rapid, hurricane-like winds that swirl faster at the equator than at the poles.

The upper layer of the atmosphere is a yellow, fog-like cloud layer made up of droplets of sulfur dioxide. The layer keeps out most of the Sun's rays, but the solar energy that does pass through the atmosphere is trapped by the thick carbon-dioxide cloud cover.

Venus also has violent lightning storms. Lightning on Venus is different from lightning on Jupiter or Earth because the electrical charges do not discharge from clouds full of water, but from clouds of sulfur dioxide.

The Greenhouse Gas Effect on Venus

Because the clouds on Venus block most of the Sun's rays, a person might assume that the planet would be cool. Instead, the clouds act as a barrier against the Sun's heat and energy that does pass through the clouds. The few rays that manage to cut through the atmosphere and reach the planet's surface can never leave. The thick carbon dioxide of the atmosphere traps the solar rays and creates Venus's extreme temperatures. Since a greenhouse is a structure that purposely traps light and heat, this trapping of heat and energy by the atmosphere is called the greenhouse gas effect.

WATER

Many scientists believe that Venus may once have had water, but they believe that it disappeared due to the relentless force of the greenhouse gas effect. The toxic atmosphere heated up the planet's surface, causing any existing water to evaporate. Once the water molecules (which are made up of hydrogen and oxygen **atoms**) vaporized into the upper atmosphere, they were divided into separate oxygen and hydrogen atoms. Hydrogen, a light gas, floated up and away from Venus's gravitational pull. The oxygen stayed in the atmosphere to create more carbon dioxide.

Some scientists theorize that there may be some water droplets left in the atmosphere of Venus. If so, they think that the atmosphere, and not the dry, hot surface, would be the most likely place to find forms of life, such as small-celled microbes.

Scientists believe that if any water exists on Venus, it is most likely high up in the planet's atmosphere.

EARTH AND VENUS

Venus is often called Earth's twin or sister planet because it is the closest in size and weight to Earth. Yet if any life-form from Earth were to visit Venus, it would be crushed by the air pressure, suffocated by toxic gases, and burned by the intense temperatures. Some scientists say Venus is really "Earth's evil twin."

Some missions to Venus have looked for proof that might show that Venus and Earth had a closer resemblance at an earlier time. Many astronomers believe that by studying Venus, they will learn more about how the Earth and the Solar System were formed. Studying Venus can also help guide scientists in managing some of Earth's present-day environmental concerns.

COMPARING VENUS AND EARTH

	VENUS	EARTH
DISTANCE FROM THE SUN	About 67.23 million miles (108 million km)	About 93 million miles (149.6 million km)
CIRCUMFERENCE	About 23,627 miles (38,025 km) at its equator	About 24,901 miles (40,075 km) at the Equator
AVERAGE SURFACE TEMPERATURE	864 degrees Fahrenheit (462 degrees C)	60 degrees Fahrenheit (15 degrees C)
LENGTH OF YEAR	224.7 Earth days	365 days
LENGTH OF DAY	243 Earth days	24 hours
NUMBER OF MOONS	No moons	1
COMPOSITION OF PLANET	Mostly metals, such as iron and nickel, and rock	Mostly metals and rock
ATMOSPHERE	Carbon dioxide, sulfur, and sulfur dioxide	Mostly nitrogen and oxygen

The Greenhouse Gas Effect on Earth

The greenhouse gas effect is a growing concern on Earth. Scientists say that burning fossil fuels like oil, gas, and coal cause greenhouse gases to develop. Carbon dioxide, a waste product of burning and one of the most harmful of the greenhouse gases, moves up into Earth's atmosphere and prevents heat from escaping. Scientists note that Earth and Venus have about the same amount of carbon dioxide. However, on Earth, organic matter such as plants, trees, and sea algae, use carbon dioxide and release oxygen as a waste gas back into the air. On Venus, there is no organic matter to absorb the carbon dioxide and so it continues to build up.

Fortunately, because there are no known life-forms on Venus, nothing suffers from the intense heat. On Earth, however, dangerous amounts of greenhouse gases will affect all of the planet's living things. By studying the greenhouse gas effect on Venus, scientists might find ways to manage or reduce the greenhouse gas buildup that is currently occurring.

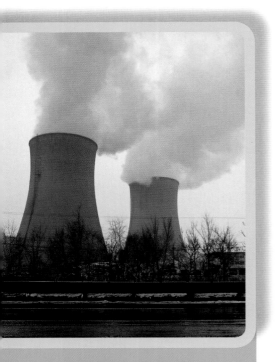

It is thought that air pollution and gaseous waste from things such as factories are causing a greenhouse gas effect on Earth.

Acid Rain

The clouds of Venus contain other toxic gases, such as sulfur and sulfur dioxide. Earth's atmosphere also contains these very acidic gases. The air on Earth becomes polluted with sulfur and sulfur dioxide when factory smoke, vehicle exhaust, and the burning of fuels such as wood, coal, oil, and natural gas, are released into the atmosphere. On Earth, the acid mixes with water droplets and falls to the ground as acid rain, smog, and dry dust. The acid destroys buildings, pollutes lakes, rivers, and soil, and suffocates animal and plant life.

On Venus, sulfur dioxide falls to the surface as a form of acid rain. The Hubble

On Earth, acid rain eats away at stone and cement structures and destroys living things, such as plants and trees. Fortunately, there is no known life to be destroyed by Venus's acid rain, which is far more acidic and deadlier than Earth's.

VENUS

Space Telescope has taken images of Venus's acid rain. Many scientists believe that Venus is slowly recovering from an intense bout of acid rain, probably caused by severe volcanic eruptions.

Many hope that learning more about Venus will someday help our own planet Earth.

On Earth, only 10 percent of the acid rain is caused by naturally occurring causes, such as volcanoes. Earth's acid rain moves around the atmosphere, damaging large regions at a time. On Venus, extreme acid rain conditions affect the entire planet.

Looking to the Future

The population on Earth has much to benefit from learning about Venus because both planets are somewhat similar in chemical composition. But the life-giving combination of water, organic life, and geology on Earth keeps our planet in balance, while Venus remains uninhabitable.

Scientists warn that the Earth's chemical balance is fragile. Many look to Venus as a critical example of what could happen if too much carbon dioxide pollution builds up in Earth's atmosphere. They say that learning more about Venus's atmosphere will help us to predict and prevent similar conditions on Earth. They hope that Earth may be able to avoid the same harsh fate as its sister planet, Venus.

QUICK FACTS ABOUT VENUS

NAME: Named after Venus, the Roman goddess of love

DISCOVERY: Known since ancient times

DISTANCE FROM THE SUN: 67,237,910 miles (108,208,930 km)

DISTANCE FROM EARTH: 25 million miles (40 million km)

LENGTH OF DAY: 243 Earth days

LENGTH OF YEAR: 224.7 Earth days

AVERAGE SURFACE TEMPERATURE: 864 degrees Fahrenheit
(462 degrees C)

NUMBER OF MOONS: None

NUMBER OF RINGS: None

GLOSSARY

atom—The basic building block of all matter.

axis—An imaginary straight line going through a planet, around which the planet rotates, or spins.

cosmic—Having to do with the universe or space.

elevation—The height of an object or landform.

elliptical—A term to describe an elongated, or egg-shaped, circle.

flyby—A space flight that travels close to a planet or moon for the purpose of making observations.

gravity—The force between objects that make them attract each other. The force of gravity increases as objects come closer together and decreases the farther apart they are.

greenhouse gas effect—The warming and planetary changes that occur when too much solar radiation is trapped by a planet's atmosphere.

Kuiper Belt—A region of the Solar System beyond Neptune that is composed of small icy bodies and comets.

landers—Spacecraft that land on a planet, moon, or other celestial body to make observations, run experiments, or retrieve samples.

NASA (National Aeronautics and Space Administration)—The United States government agency responsible for aerospace research and space flight.

orbit—The path taken by a celestial body, such as a planet or moon.

orbiter—A spacecraft that orbits a planet or a moon in the Solar System.

probe—Any kind of spacecraft designed to explore extraterrestrial objects and send back data to Earth.

supernova—The huge explosion of a star at the end of its life, which releases a massive amount of energy and produces extremely bright light.

terra—A continent-like land mass on a planet.

transit—The passage of a smaller astronomical body in front of a larger one. Only Mercury and Venus pass between the Earth and the Sun.

FIND OUT MORE

BOOKS

Aguilar, David. *Planets, Stars, and Galaxies: A Visual Encyclopedia of Our Universe.* Washington, D.C.: National Geographic Society, 2008.

Asimov, Isaac, and Richard Hantula. *Exploring Outer Space.* Milwaukee, WI: Gareth Stevens, 2006.

Barnes-Svarney, Patricia. *A Traveler's Guide to the Solar System.* New York, NY: Sterling Publishing, 2008.

Carson, Mary Kay. *Exploring the Solar System: A History with 22 Activities.* Chicago: Chicago Review Press, 2008.

Crosswell, Ken. *Ten Worlds: Everything that Orbits the Sun.* Honesdale, PA: Boyds Mills Press, 2007.

Elkins-Tanton, Linda T. *The Sun, Mercury, and Venus.* New York: Chelsea House, 2006.

Feinstein, Stephen. *Venus.* Berkeley Heights, NJ: MyReportLinks.com Books, 2005.

Goss, Tim. *Venus.* Chicago: Heinemann Library, 2008.

Graham, Ian. *The Near Planets.* Mankato, MN: Smart Apple Media, 2007.

Renfield, R. K. *Venus.* New York: Rosen Publishing, 2005.

Rooney, Anne. *Outer Space.* Chicago: Heinemann Library, 2007.

WEBSITES

Cool Cosmos: Venus
http://coolcosmos.ipac.caltech.edu/cosmic_kids/AskKids/venus.shtml

Curious about Astronomy? Ask an Astronomer
http://curious.astro.cornell.edu

Explore Venus
http://www.kidscosmos.org/kid-stuff/venus-facts.html

NASA Kids' Club
http://www.nasa.gov/audience/forkids/kidsclub/flash/index.html

NASA Solar System Exploration for Kids
http://solarsystem.nasa.gov/kids/index.cfm

NASA—Venus
http://www.nasa.gov/worldbook/venus_worldbook.html

The Space Place
http://spaceplace.nasa.gov/en/kids

Transits of Venus
http://eclipse.gsfc.nasa.gov/transit/catalog/VenusCatalog.html

Venus Exploration Timeline
http://nssdc.gsfc.nasa.gov/planetary/chronology_venus.html

Venus: Explore the Cosmos
http://www.planetary.org/explore/topics/venus

Venus Express
http://sci.esa.int/science-e/www/area/index.cfm?fareaid=64

BIBLIOGRAPHY

The author found these resources especially helpful while researching this book.

Astronomy and Astrophysics, Tufts University. "Unveiling Venus—The Global Perspective." http://www.tufts.edu/as/astronomy/LangChap4a.html

Boyd, Jay. "Hot Climate Could Shut Down Plate Tectonics." http://www.eurekalert.org/pub_releases/2008-05/ru-hcc051208.php

Corfield, R. M. *Lives of the Planets: A Natural History of the Solar System.* New York: Basic Books, 2007.

Cattermole, Peter John. *Venus, the Geological Story*. Baltimore: Johns Hopkins University Press, 1994.

"Gamma-Ray Telescopes & Detectors." http://imagine.gsfc.nasa.gov/docs/science/how_l2/gamma_detectors.html

Grinspoon, David Harry. *Venus Revealed: A New Look Below the Clouds of our Mysterious Twin Planet.* Reading, MA: Addison-Wesley Pub., 1997.

Journal of Archaeology, History, and Exploration. "Impact Craters on Venus, Earth, and Other Planets." http://www.athenapub.com/venus1.htm

McFadden, Lucy-Ann Adams, ed. *Encyclopedia of the Solar System.* Boston: Academic, 2007.

NASA Eclipse. http://eclipse.gsfc.nasa.gov/transit/transit.html

Science Daily—Solar System News. http://www.sciencedaily.com/news/space_time/solar_system/

Sparrow, Giles. *The Planets: A Journey Through the Solar System*. London: Quercus, 2006.

University Corporation for Atmospheric Research-University of Michigan. "Windows to the Universe." http://www.windows.ucar.edu/tour/link=/venus/venus.html&edu=high

INDEX

Page numbers in **boldface** indicate
    photos or illustrations.

VENUS

ABOUT THE AUTHOR

Ruth Bjorklund lives on Bainbridge Island, near Seattle, Washington. One of her favorite things to do at the end of the day is to walk her dogs in the park and enjoy the bright glow of Venus in the early night sky.